Curious George
Gymnastics Fun

Adaptation by Leora Bernstein
Based on the TV series teleplay written by Bill Burnett

Houghton Mifflin Harcourt
Boston New York

For information about permission to reproduce selections from this book, write to Permissions, Houghton Mifflin Harcourt Publishing Company, 215 Park Avenue South, New York, New York 10003.

ISBN: 978-0-544-43056-3 paper-over-board
ISBN: 978-0-544-43057-0 paperback

Design by Afsoon Razavi

www.hmhco.com

Printed in China
SCP 10 9 8 7 6 5 4 3 2 1
4500507736

AGES	GRADES	GUIDED READING LEVEL	READING RECOVERY LEVEL	LEXILE ® LEVEL
5–7	1	I	15–16	270L

Today was George's first gymnastics class!
His friends Allie and Bill were in class,
too.

The gym looked
like a playground.
George wanted to try everything!

The teacher said they had to stretch first.
"There are three *S* rules in gymnastics,"
she said.
Stretching was the first *S* rule.

They stretched high.
They stretched low.

Supervision was *S* rule number two.
Allie balanced on the balance beam.
The teacher supervised.

Bill wanted to try the rings.
They were hard!
"Gymnasts must be really strong,"
said Bill.

"You have to build muscles," the
teacher said.
Until then, she gave him a bench for safety.
Safety was the third *S* rule.

Soon class was over.
"Great job! See you next week," the
teacher said.

Next week?
George could not wait that long.
He wanted to practice every day.

"If I owned a gym, it would always be open!" Bill said.

That gave George an idea.
They could make their own gym!

First, they needed mats so they
could stretch.
George found sleeping bags in the
basement.

George took them outside.
He put one bag on top of the other bag.
Now they were as soft as the gym mats.

"What about a balance beam?" Allie asked.
The fence would be a good balance beam.

But it was too high.
It would not be safe.
They put a wood beam from
the fence on the ground.

Bill wanted some rings.
They had to be just the right size.
Shower curtain rings were too small.

But towel rings were perfect!

George tied them to the tree.
Bill still needed lots of practice.

Their gym was ready.
Now Allie, Bill, and George could
practice every day!
And they did.

The next week, they went back to class.
The teacher was amazed at their
progress.
They were gym-tastic!

A Recipe for Success

Gymnasts need fuel! And what's better fuel than a delicious and filling snack? This recipe will keep you jumping for joy and swinging around all day!

No-Bake Energy Balls

What you will need:
1 ¼ cup of old-fashioned oats
⅔ cup toasted coconut flakes
½ cup peanut butter
½ cup chocolate chips
⅓ cup honey or maple syrup
1 tsp. vanilla extract

Instructions:
1) Mix all the ingredients together in a medium bowl until thoroughly mixed.
2) Cover the bowl and put it in the refrigerator for half an hour.
3) Roll the dough into balls.
4) Enjoy a healthy snack! Share the rest with friends or store them in the refrigerator for later.

Suggestion: You can make this with dried fruits, candy, or nuts instead of chocolate chips! Use your imagination to try different kinds of No-Bake Energy Balls!

Gym-tag-tics

Fitness can be a lot of fun! Practice your skills at home with this exciting game!

What you will need:
Construction paper
Safety pins
Any writing instrument (marker, crayon, pencil)

What to do:
On the construction paper, write one gymnastics skill for each player.

Some ideas:
Stretch
Balance on one foot
Somersault
Cartwheel

Safety-pin each piece of construction paper on a player (if you have more than four people, you can write the skills more than once).

The player with "stretch" on his or her tag will be "it" first.

Now, play tag! But when someone gets tagged, he has to do what is on the construction paper of whoever is "it."

If a skill is too hard, you can do 10 jumping jacks instead.

After 5 minutes, switch whoever is "it."